Level

W9-CFJ-622

Bill Martin's

INSTANT READERS

LEVEL 3   TEACHER'S GUIDE

Holt, Rinehart and Winston, Inc.

New York　　*Toronto*　　*London*　　*Sydney*

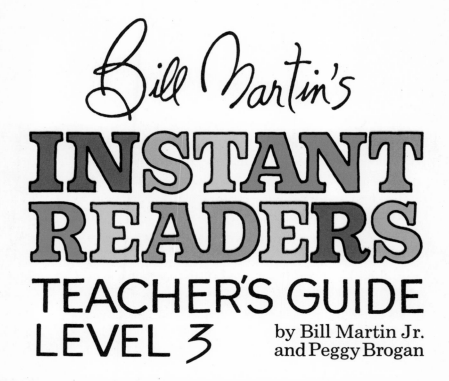

Bill Martin's

INSTANT READERS

TEACHER'S GUIDE
LEVEL 3

by Bill Martin Jr.
and Peggy Brogan

CONTENTS

INTRODUCTION

PART 1

Rationale of the InstantReader Program

PART 2

Discussion of each title in the series

(continued)

(continued)

PART 3

Follow-up activities for Level 3 books

INSTANT READERS

LEVEL 3 Teacher's Guide

Letter from Bill Martin Jr.

INTRODUCTION

Dear friends,

The *InstantReaders* are an integral part
of the Bill Martin language-literature offerings
and therefore embody the basic philosophy
already spelled out in the *Sounds of Language* readers
and in the *Owl Books.*
The *InstantReaders*, however, especially focus
in new exciting ways
on the use of structure as a decoding skill
and the use of dependably structured books
in releasing children immediately to visions of themselves
as successful-and-pleasured readers.
It is this cover-to-cover immediacy,
along with esthetic and linguistic intrigue,
that makes the *InstantReaders* uniquely impressive
in a child's reading career.
No matter what kinds of reading materials
you are using in your classroom,
these books will add their own special dimensions by

1) instilling children with the belief that they can read
and at the same time providing them with materials
that support that belief,
2) cultivating joyous familiarity with a corps of language models
and book experiences
that serve as a leavening to skill acquisition,
3) incorporating sensitivities to structure
(rhyme, rhythm, phrase-sentence-and-story patterns)
for purposes of decoding,
4) capitalizing upon familiar linguistic and cultural structures
in launching children into reading,
5) involving children esthetically (as well as intellectually)
in the printed page,
6) holding wholebook*success* as a basic purpose
of reading instruction.

Bill Martin Jr.

Three levels of InstantReaders

Level 1
Brown Bear, Brown Bear, What Do You See?
When It Rains, It Rains
A Ghost Story
The Haunted House
Silly Goose and the Holidays
I Went to the Market
Fire! Fire! Said Mrs. McGuire
The Wizard
Monday, Monday, I Like Monday
Up and Down the Escalator

Level 2
Whistle, Mary, Whistle
A Spooky Story
City Song
Old Mother Middle-Muddle
The Longest Journey in the World
King of the Mountain
Old Devil Wind
The Little Disaster
Tatty Mae and Catty Mae
I'm Going to Build a Supermarket One of These Days

Level 3
Ten Little Squirrels
"Tricks or Treats?"
Welcome Home, Henry
The Maestro Plays
The Happy Hippopotami
My Days are Made of Butterflies
What to Say and When to Say It
The Turning of the Year
I Paint the Joy of a Flower
The Eagle Has Landed

INSTANT READERS

LEVEL 3 Teacher's Guide

Rationale of the InstantReader Program

PART 1

ON the very **FIRST DAY** of **1ST** grade,

Children in our society inherit the need to read. They also inherit the expectancy that they will read a book the first day of first grade. When they don't, they go home disappointed—and the first breach between a child and reading success has been created.

How much better to invite those "first-dayers" to hear a highly structured book that they immediately can "read back" cover-to-cover. *Children, isn't this wonderful! Here it is only the first day of first grade and already you can read a book!* The *InstantReader* program is designed to fulfill this cultural need for you and children. The *InstantReaders* are reading readiness at its best. They put a flow of language in children's ears and eyes and mouth, and fill their lives with the radiance of reading success.

every child
should have a book
that he can
joyfully read
from cover
to cover

THE FIRST

reading skill is the belief,

and most basic

"I can read a book"

Over the years teachers, lacking surefire beginning books, have been forced to engage children in all sorts of reading readiness materials that have no connection whatsoever with a book, and sometimes even less with language. Consequently, children have been denied for six or more weeks fulfillment of their strong urge to read a book. Since six weeks can be a long time in a young child's life, all too many begin their reading careers by losing the urge to read and even by becoming confused about the act of reading. *Children, would you like to read another book today? Here it is only the second day of first grade and already you can read two books!* What better way to insure the reading success of a child than to send him home proudly declaring, *I can read! I can read!* This pervasive belief in himself as a reader is the underlying skill for his acquisition of all other reading skills.

The book is a cultural symbol of man's becoming. Our lives are shot through with evidence of this phenomenon: when we are cut off from book *success*, we feel less than worthy; to the contrary, we feel pleasured and proud having books around the house; we are more pleased with children when they spend time with books than when they spend time with TV; we brag to each other about the books we have read and are going to read; *etc*.

Unfortunately, traditional reading instruction has never given wholebook*success* its proper emphasis. Rather it has set up an endless succession

BOOK EXPERIENCE *should precede* **WORD EXPERIENCE** *in bringing a child to print*

of hurdles, largely word oriented, that children must master, with very little concern for wholebook*success*. The *InstantReader* program, by contrast, provides wholebook*success* concomitantly with reading instruction. It makes the reading of entire books initially available to children through the ear, and gives them the constant support of the book symbol and its aura of well-being as they engage in the sticky details of skillbuilding. *Boys and girls, isn't this exciting! Just look at the big pile of books you already can read.*

14

The longer and more complex a child's reading assignments become, the more he needs a collection of short, beautifully structured books that appeal to his imagination, his esthetic yearnings, and his reading prowess. The *InstantReaders* offer three levels of books to satisfy these needs. *The levels must not be confused with grade levels.*

The levels with their ordinal designations simply suggest the comparative complexity of language patterns and symbolisms. Lucky is the child who has available all three levels so that he can wander back and forth at will, finding out about his tastes in art and language, his needs for books that he can read in a few minutes, his yen for humor to leaven the more serious parts of his day, his joy in quick success: *I can do it! I can do it! I can do it!* In the midst of struggling with fractions or remedial reading, for example, a child can restore his belief in himself by picking up a book that has pretensions to linguistic excellence and still can be mastered *inside and out*.

a child has continuing need for whole book success throughout his reading career

15

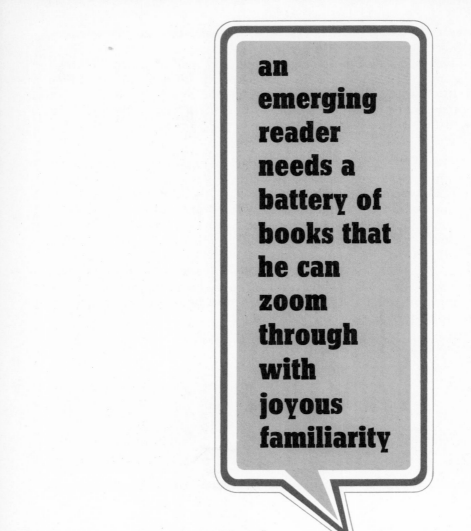

an emerging reader needs a battery of books that he can zoom through with joyous familiarity

Every child, particularly in the early reaches of reading instruction, needs a battery of books that he can "read on his own" for personal pleasure. Too many times children spend an entire semester learning to read a single book, then even before they have had the pleasure of returning to it time and again, "just for fun," they are hurried on to the next reader. As important as choosing books from the library can be, this does not take the place in the young reader's life of having constantly available a corps of favorite books that can be read without any awareness of word/unlocking problems. Taste is not formed by being hurried from book to book, but rather by knowing which book you want to return to again and again, and by knowing which sentences, which pictures, which words you like better than others. Those of us who seriously care about helping children learn to read might question what we accomplish by teaching the so-called reading skills if we "turn out" children who don't of their own volition reach/out for books. Joyous familiarity with a corps of select books is probably the greatest motivation factor in nurturing a developing reader.

young readers need the thrust of literary fellowship

The literary fellowship engendered by continuous exposure to a collection of books that are being read and enjoyed and discussed in a variety of circumstances and settings is the milieu in which sensitive and mature readers thrive. Imagine the delight of a child who cocks an ear and hears two friends reading aloud *Whistle, Mary, Whistle,* an old favorite of his. Or imagine the glow of awareness children have when a teacher paraphrases Old Mother Middle Muddle, "Now ... let's see ... what were we going to do? ... O, yes ... now I remember ... we were going to go home."

Consider, in contrast, the divisive competitive overtones in a classroom where certain books belong only to the "high" reading group, others to the "low." And consider the unhealthy emotional atmosphere when two good friends can't share the same books because they are divided by reading groups or reading levels. The *InstantReaders* cut across such levels and belong to all children in a classroom. Not that *every* child must read *every* book, but that his reading career needs the stretch and comfort and human enjoyment of a commonly/shared corps of literature.

DRAMATIC CUMULATIVE REPETITIONS OF LANGUAGE

help children anticipate (and thereby decode) the printed page

Most of the *InstantReaders* have obvious repetitive struc-tures which immediately propel children into anticipating the next line or the next rhyming word or the next episode. Naturally this is not an infallible method of decoding print, but it is one impressive experience in helping children know that they can trust print because of its underlying structures.

In a dark dark woods there is a dark dark house,

In the dark dark house there is a dark dark stair,

Down the dark dark stair . . .

Even on first acquaintance, a child will predict that

1) the pattern of this phrasing will maintain throughout the story,
2) that all of the objects will be described as *dark dark*,
3) that the last part of each line becomes the first part of the next line.

Imagine the child's surprise, therefore, to discover that the *spirit* in the dark dark bottle is not *dark dark*, but is *evil*. Couched as this variation is within so many dependable repetitions, it does not cause a child to lose faith in his method of predicting language, but rather suggests to him that there are also other methods of decoding language that will be helpful. His curiosity, therefore, is piqued to find multiple ways of unlocking print. *Children, isn't it interesting that the author didn't call the spirit dark dark. How can you tell by looking at the print that he did not say dark dark?*

language skills are best learned in the shape and swing of a sentence

Children intuitively know that language is best learned in the shape and swing of sentences. This is how they learned to talk. Most five-year-olds already own a wide range of sentence structures. If, however, a child doesn't have a sufficient repertoire of oral language structures, the school's first job is to enter them into his ear in such enticing ways that he will reach out to claim them as his own. The sentence patterns in the *InstantReaders*, sharply focused by predictable story structure, range from the simplest noun-verb construction, *I sing*, to the highly complex pattern, "*O joy!*" said the fox, "*when the rooster comes out to swallow the bee, I'll grab him by the neck.*" Complicated though this latter sentence may seem, couched as it is within the dependable structure of the book, it is more easily available to children than oversimplified sentences that are not couched in dependable story structure.

dependable
schemes of
rhyme
and
rhythm
help children
read words they
didn't know they knew

WILMARTH SCHOOL
ASHLAND, WIS.

Just as children intake oral language more easily when it is in rhyme-y or jingle-y form, so they find themselves more at ease with storybooks of similar design. Having perceived that a story rhymes in couplets or in alternate lines, children are strongly prepared to speak and to read the rhyming words throughout the story, even before they can handle the rest of the phrasing: *I dance. I sing.*
I run. I wing.
I skip. I jump.
I hop. I hump.
This type of rhyme scheme is a child's most reliable clue for handling the dance of words in this story. The word *hump*, for example, falls easily into place in spite of its unusualness. The rhyme and rhythm pattern dictates that the word must be a one-syllable word rhyming with *jump*. As the child goes further into reading and learns about beginning consonants, short vowel sounds, and the usefulness of configuration and picture clues, he will bring any or all of these into play as he unlocks an unknown rhyming word, but it nonetheless is the rhyming clue that undergirds his whole decoding process.

The recognition of a rhyming word within literary structure is qualitatively different from studying isolated lists of rhyming words. Literary structure gives the word a linguistic mooring and integrity that it can never achieve in isolation. Interestingly enough, an experience of this kind may subsequently trigger children into making lists of rhyming words, but this activity is permeated with the awareness that isolated words are dead things and need the thrust of linguistic structure to claim their being. It is this kind of knowledge gleaned from *InstantReader* experiences that contributes significantly to a child's emerging generalizations about language and how it works.

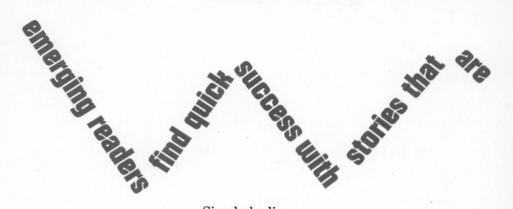
emerging readers find quick success with stories that are

Simply by liv-
ing in our cul-
ture, children have
certain built-in struc-
tures going for them that
can be translated to advantage in learning to read. They
know, for example, that the hours
of the day, the days of the week, the
months and seasons of the year, the number system, and the alphabet have dependable sequences. Sooner or later the children
become familiar with and use these sequences
like another hand or foot or eye or ear in dealing with
the outside world. The *Instant Reader* program exploits
certain of these structures as another way to help children
appreciate the fact that the recognition of underlying structure

patterned on familiar cultural sequences

is an aid in decoding print. *Sunday, Sunday, I like Sunday, Sunday the first day of the week. Monday, Monday, I Like Monday, Monday the second day of the week. . . .* From this point in the story, a child needs only his knowledge of ordinal numbers to 7, and the names and sequence of the days of the week to read seven spreads of print. The intrigue of the last half of the book, *Monday, Monday* in which these familiar structures are reversed and in other ways played upon, highlights in intriguing ways the usefulness of familiar structures in unlocking unfamiliar new print.

remedial reading should begin with every child role-playing himself as a

At whatever time a child is assigned to remedial reading, he needs immediately to know that he can read an entire book. Chances are that he has plodded through month after month of reading instruction, never having the feeling of wholebook*success*. The *Instant-Readers* provide the opportunity for a sharp turnabout in that detrimental course of action. A child can, in fact, read an entire book on the very first day. Luckily there is nothing "firstgradish" or "scaled vocabulary-ish" about the *Instant Readers*. Many fifth graders who are offended, for example, by scaled down stories about fake cowboys will pit all of their intuitions toward figuring out the author's scheme of putting *Silly Goose and the Holidays* together, sensing

successful reader of books

that the author was interested in a literary outcome and not an easy-vocabulary manipulation. The integrity of the literary structure of *Silly Goose* comes through at whatever age the reader. Moreover, the *InstantReaders* free a child from the grip of having only a single word-unlocking skill (sounding out the word) and help him add a wide ranging repertoire of structural decoding skills to what he already possesses. *Boys and girls, this may look like an easy book to you, but we're going to do fifthgrade things with it. How long has it been since you figured out the scheme an author had in mind when he put his book together? Figuring out the scheme of a story may be one of your most useful reading skills.* You will be surprised at how fast a child grasps the awareness that he can read.

when a book involves a child **E**sthetically its message has more meaning.

Esthetic involvement touches you "where you live." It defies convention and logic and academic know-how, yet it has everything to do with learning because it wells out of a person's strivings for human kinship. The ingenuous, cumulative coupling of sequences in *Brown Bear, Brown Bear,* is an example:

Brown bear, brown bear, what do you see?
I see a redbird looking at me.
Redbird, redbird, what do you see?
I see a yellow duck looking at me.
Yellow duck, yellow duck, what do you see?
I see a blue horse looking at me, etc.

The coupling has nothing and yet everything to do with reading. Momentarily banished are the restrictions of print, the preoccupation with eye movements from left to right, and "today's new words" drill. The literature creates its own life. The linguistic dance of the question and answer in *Brown Bear* is so pervasive and appealing that the reader is caught up in it and responds without labored awareness of technicalities and rules. And consider the delight and *pulling-power* of *Tricks or Treats?* which playfully rewrites jelly beans as *belly jeans*, lollipops as *pollilops*, popcorn balls as *copborn palls*, all in intriguing sweeps of language which twist and curlicue and bend back upon themselves as part of the pictorial design. The important meanings of these and other *InstantReaders* are not the story facts. It is irrelevant which animal Brown Bear saw or what trick was performed on which floor of the apartment house. The humanly worthwhile meanings are found in the playfulness of the language, in the interrelations of color and design and story evolvements, and in the inculcated awareness that life is worth living.

"Read-along" cassettes and L.P. recordings, adding insightful and memorable linguistic dimensions to each of the *Instant Readers,* are now available. These are the first recordings that Bill Martin, America's distinguished storyteller and creator of provocative oral-aural reading materials, has made for classroom use. As you can imagine from knowing Bill Martin's *Owl Books, Sounds of Language Reader's,* and now the *Instant Readers,* his "read-along" recordings involve children esthetically, linguistically and humanly in the miracle of man's greatest invention—language. Your children will be reading along with Bill Martin, responding to and inculcating his love of language—all the while learning how to read with accuracy, joy and security. As their eyes see what their ears hear and their tongues speak, children will deposit into their linguistic storehouses, model sentence and story patterns that evoke pervasive skill development in all of the language arts—reading, writing, speaking, and listening.

INSTANT READERS

LEVEL 3 Teacher's Guide

Discussion of each book

PART 2

Ten Little Squirrels

an old rhyme adapted by Bill Martin Jr.
with pictures by Bernard Martin

Ten little squirrels
Played in a tree.

The first one said,
"What do I see?"

The second one said,
"A man with a gun."

The third one said,
"We'd better run."

The fourth one said,
"Let's hide in the shade."

The fifth one said,
"I'm not afraid."

The sixth one said,
"Don't make a sound."

The seventh one said,
"He's looking all around."

The eighth one said,
"Let's run to our nest."

The ninth one said,
"No, staying here is best."

The tenth one sneezed . . .
"Ker . . . ker . . . ker . . . ker . . . KERCHOO!!"

Then B A N G went the gun,

And ten little squirrels,
How they did run!

Ten Little Squirrels is hung together with ordinal number, a rhyme scheme and one of those adding-on plot structures where one thing happens after another until something brings the whole thing to an end. Children may remember a shortened version of this adapted rhyme from earlier childhood days. Whether or not they do, they will soon be chiming in with you as you read, proving to themselves once again, *I can read a whole book from cover to cover.* Any or all of the follow-up activities described in Part III of this teacher's guide can be used with *Ten Little Squirrels.* A few that are especially worth pursuing are discussed here.

1. **Reading joyfully from cover to cover,** p. 76. In no time the children will be imitating the ten little squirrels in their choral reading of the book. It will be interesting to discuss which kinds of character traits they wish to portray in the various squirrels' lines.

2. **Innovating on literary structure,** p. 77. and **Analyzing**
3. **literary structure,** p. 79. By the time the children have read through the third little squirrel, they will have caught the author's plan and can try their own versions of similar plans for putting a story together.

> *Six funny boys*
> *Were singing a song.*
>
> *The first one said,*
> *"Something must be wrong."*

As the children experiment with and discuss the underlying structure of *Ten Little Squirrels,* you might feel that this is a productive time to help the children generalize the fact that an understanding of literary structure in any story or poem helps a person read words he did not know he knew. Intuitively, children know how useful structure can be in figuring out vocabulary because they use it so often when they are on their own in reading and no one is telling them they must "sound out" each unknown word. Once they have verbalized this intuitive knowledge about the usefulness of structure, it becomes more available to them as an aware decoding skill.

5. **Analyzing sentence structure,** p. 87. If children seem to be having problems in their independent story writing getting sentences involving conversation written down with useful punctuation, this story abounds in model sentences punctuated to show conversation. Transforming any one of the basic sentences may clear up problems children have been encountering in their writing or reading.

8. **Responding to art,** p. 95. You and the children can have a great time discussing the symbolism in the art in *Ten Little Squirrels.* Invite the children to search the paintings for evidence that the story concerns more than just a few passing moments in the lives of ten specific squirrels and one specific hunter.

Isn't it interesting, for example, that the art spans sunrise to sunset and season to season, rather than just a few moments? Isn't it interesting that the hunter is faceless. Supposing the ten little squirrels represent all wild life and the hunter represents the constant rather than the momentary threat to wild life, then what meanings does the story have?

Or, supposing the squirrels represent all living things, including people, and the hunter represents a threat to living things, now what kinds of meanings does the story evoke? Once they have tested the satisfaction in this kind of reading of *Ten Little Squirrels,* they may wish to return to it again and again, looking for more symbolism. And they may wish to turn to other stories and pictures to enjoy their new skill. How nice!

"Tricks or Treats?"

by Bill Martin Jr. illustrated by Jim Spanfeller
handlettering by Ray Barber

Down to the ninth floor.
Knock on Knicker Knocker's door.
"Tricks or treats?"
"Tricks," says Knicker Knocker.
So I change into a Knocker Knicker.

Down to the eighth floor.
Knock on Slipper Slopper's door.
"Tricks or treats?"
"Tricks," says Slipper Slopper.
So I change into a Slopper Slipper.

Down to the seventh floor.
Knock on Fiddle Faddle's door.
"Tricks or treats?"
"Tricks," says Fiddle Faddle.
So I change into a Faddle Fiddle.

Down to the sixth floor.
Knock on Dripper Dropper's door.
"Tricks or treats?"
"Tricks," says Dripper Dropper.
So I change into a Dropper Dripper.

Down to the fifth floor.
Knock on Wiffle Waffle's door.
"Tricks or treats?"
"Tricks," says Wiffle Waffle.
So I change into a Waffle Wiffle.

Down to the fourth floor.
Knock on Teeter Totter's door.
"Tricks or treats?"
"Tricks," says Teeter Totter.
So I change into a Totter Teeter.

Down to the third floor.
Knock on Snicker Snacker's door.
"Tricks or treats?"
"Tricks," says Snicker Snacker.
So I change into a Snacker Snicker.

Down to the second floor.
Knock on Wiggle Waggle's door.
"Tricks or treats?"
"Tricks," says Wiggle Waggle.
So I change into a Waggle Wiggle.

Down to the first floor.
Knock on Pumper Nickel's door.
"Tricks or treats?"
"Tricks," says Pumper Nickel.
So I change into a Nickle Pumper.

Down to the basement.
Knock on the ceiling.
"Hey, you huuuumans up there . . .
. . . . SPOOKS get huuuuuunnnngry,
tooooooooooooo!"

Up to the first floor . . . .
Knock on Pumper Nickel's door. . . .
Pumper Nickel gives pollilops.
Up to the second floor.
Knock on Wiggle Waggle's door.
Wiggle Waggle gives gewing chum.
Up to the third floor.
Knock on Snicker Snacker's door.
Snicker Snacker gives bandy cars and neaputs.
Up to the fourth floor,
Knock on Teeter Totter's door.
Teeter Totter gives dumgrops.
Up to the fifth floor.
Knock on Wiffle Waffle's door.
Wiffle Waffle gives Jackercracks.
Up to the sixth floor.
Knock on Dripper Dropper's door.
Dripper Dropper gives papples and nabanas.
Up to the seventh floor.
Knock on Fiddle Faddle's door.
Fiddle Faddle gives belly jeans.
Up to the eighth floor.
Knock on Slipper Slopper's door.
Slipper Slopper gives copborn palls.
Up to the ninth floor.
Knock on Knicker Knocker's door.
Knicker Knocker gives capecuks and noughduts.
YUM YUM YUM
chomp! chomp! chomp!
DELICIOUSDELICIOUSDELICIOUS
chew . . . chew . . . chew . . .
slurp . . . slurp . . . slurp . . .

Tricks Or Treats has a lot of structure that can be counted on. To begin with, there's a lot of dependable repetition. There's also a dependable (although zany!) language pattern. And there is ordinal number, both forward and backward. Any of the follow-up activities described in Part III can be used with *Tricks Or Treats?* A few that are especially worth pursuing are discussed here.

1. **Reading joyfully from cover to cover,** p. 76. By the time the spooky character is down to the seventh floor, the children will be chiming in. Encourage the children to use their spookiest voices along with whatever sound effects they can invent to add to the atmosphere. When children are reading aloud and depositing literary and language structures in their linguistic storehouses, the more dramatic the reading, the more firmly are the patterns planted.

2. **Innovating on literary structure,** p. 77, and **Analyzing**
3. **literary structure,** p. 79. Children have many choices as they plan innovations on *Tricks Or Treats?* The "Tricks or treats?" line may intrigue them, and some may try their hands at creating stories around "April Fool." Others may change the basic pattern of movement to an escalator or even to a space ship going from planet to planet. Whatever innovations they create, they will have a chance to see that their new stories read more easily because they are familiar with the underlying structures. Little by little children verbalize these kinds of insight and thereby claim them as their own.

6. Analyzing word structure, p. 90. What fun the children will have with the word-play in this book! One of the best ways to discover that the shapes of words can importantly affect their pronunciation, is to encounter these intriguing kinds of reversals.

Slipper Slopper   Slopper Slipper
Dum grops   Belly jeans   Nabanas

7. Responding to typographical intrigue, p. 93. As the type moves in and out and around with the art, the children discover in impressive ways that printed language is a puzzle which reveals its secrets to the person who figures out how it works. Once the children are intrigued with the many ways type can move, they may be ready to generalize the fact that in the English language, type moves from left to right most of the time.

8. Responding to art, p. 95. Jim Spanfeller has chosen a symbolic rather than a realistic treatment of this familiar Hallowe'en theme. The mystery is heightened by the abstract art. As the children discuss their reactions, they may enjoy discovering that the eyes and mouth are the only living things actually seen on the pages of the book. They may also enjoy discussing why the artist didn't feel that it was necessary to paint an apartment house setting for the story. Their reactions to the play between the names of the people visited and the art (the suggested drops on Dripper Dropper's page, for example) may invite some interesting experimentation.

Welcome Home, Henry

by Bill Martin Jr. with pictures by Muriel Batherman

Said Mother in a loud voice that carried downstairs to the front door,
    IS THAT YOU, HENRY?
Said Henry in a quiet voice that didn't carry upstairs,
    YEAH, I'M HOME.

Said Mother in a louder voice that carried downstairs
and filled the living room,
    ANSWER ME, HENRY.
Said Henry in a louder voice that carried upstairs,
    I DID!

Said Mother in a loud voice that carried downstairs,
    YOU DID WHAT?
Said Henry in a quiet voice that carried upstairs,
    I ANSWERED YOU.

Said Mother in her loudest voice that carried all through the house,
    HENRY, YOU'RE TRACKING MUD AGAIN!
Said Henry in a quiet voice that carried upstairs,
    NO, I'M NOT.

Said Mother in a loud voice that carried downstairs,
    CLEAN YOUR SHOES ANYWAY.
Said Henry in a quiet voice that carried upstairs,
    WHAT?

Said Mother in a louder voice that carried downstairs,
    CLEAN YOUR SHOES ANYWAY! THEY MUST BE MUDDY!
Said Henry in a quiet voice that carried upstairs,
    O.K., MOM.

Said Mother in a loud voice that carried downstairs
where Henry was turning on the TV,
>   DON'T TURN ON THE TV, HENRY!
Said Henry in a quiet voice that carried upstairs,
>   WHY NOT?

Said Mother in a loud voice that carried downstairs,
>   BECAUSE YOU'RE BEING PUNISHED, REMEMBER?
>   ! (said Henry)

Said Mother in a loud voice that carried downstairs and into the kitchen
where Henry was about to finger the cake,
>   HENRY, STAY AWAY FROM THAT CAKE!

Said Mother in her loudest voice that carried downstairs and into the kitchen
where Henry was fingering the cake,
>   I SAID STAY AWAY FROM THAT CAKE, HENRY! IT'S FOR SUPPER!
>   THEN WHAT'S TO EAT?

Said Mother in a loud voice that carried downstairs and into the kitchen
where Henry was still fingering the cake,
>   THERE'S A GLASS OF BUTTERMILK IN THE REFRIGERATOR.
>   THANKS FOR NOTHIN'.

Said Mother in a loud voice that carried downstairs and into the kitchen
where Henry was digging into a box of raisins,
>   HOW WAS SCHOOL TODAY, DEAR?
>   FINE.

Said Mother in a loud voice that carried downstairs through the house
and into the basement where Henry was getting his ball glove,
>   WHAT DID YOU LEARN IN SCHOOL TODAY, DEAR?
Said Henry in a loud voice,
>   NOTHIN'.

Said Mother in a loud voice that carried downstairs and out into the
yard where Henry was looking for a ball game,
>   IT'S NICE TO HAVE YOU HOME, DEAR.
>   IT'S NICE TO BE HOME, MOM!

As the children listen to *Welcome Home, Henry*, they will recognize it as a spoof on the kinds of conversations that frequently go on between mothers and children. They may be so reminded of their own conversations that they will burst into spontaneous talk. Give them time for this spontaneous responding, as this is one sure way to help children know that reading a book is personally rewarding.

1. **Reading joyfully from cover to cover,** p. 78. Here is a book for choral reading, perhaps with the girls reading Mother's part, the boys reading Henry's part, and you reading the narrator's lines. The boys may want a practice session to figure out what all Henry is saying in that backwards type.

2. **Innovating on literary structure,** p. 79 and **Analyzing literary structure,** p. 81. The dependability of the pattern
3. in this story invites innovating with any two characters who are likely to be involved in a steady stream of conversation. Children's choices of characters have ranged all the way from a big sister and her boy friend to Rick Ranger and Smokey Bear. If the children wish to turn their oral innovations into books, you can help a lot by taking down what they say and giving them this copy to work from in doing their actual writing. And please don't be worried if the children laboriously write backwards for one of their characters just as Bill Martin did for Henry. This is one exciting way for focussing on the printed form of language and figuring out how it works. As the children plan their own variations on *Welcome Home, Henry*, they can be helped to verbalize their observations about how the author put his story together.

4. **Analyzing rhythmical structure,** p. 86, and **Analyzing**
5. **sentence structure,** p. 87. If the children read any of the
conversations between Mother and Henry, saying *duh* for
each syllable rather than saying words, they will soon perceive
that there is a definite rhythmical structure underlying these
sentences. As they experiment with the sound of the sentences, they can also be invited to make observations about
the ways the author put his sentences together. How do they
like his way for reversing the usual word order (Said Mother)?
Do they notice the reliable cluster of words beginning with the
word *that* following the word *voice* in each sentence? These
sentences are profitable ones for transforming, since the children's vocabulary substitutions and resultant new sentences
will provoke discussion about the shape of the sentences.

7. **Responding to typographical intrigue,** p. 92, and
8. **Responding to art,** p. 94. Open to any page of this book,
and there is esthetic intrigue created by the use of art and
type. How do the children like the artist's way for showing
the relative locations of Henry and Mother in the house? And
how do they like her use of cut-out colored paper? How do
they like the use of backward type to suggest the movement
of Henry's voice and the use of forward type to suggest the
movement of Mother's voice? What a profitable time to invite
the children to experiment with some page designing of their
own, using both art and arrangements of words to create the
message they want to create.

The Maestro Plays

by Bill Martin Jr. pictures by Sal Murdocca
handlettering by Ray Barber

The maestro plays.
He plays proudly.
He plays loudly.
He plays slowly
He plays Ohly.
He plays reachingly.
He plays beseechingly.
He plays flowingly
    glowingly . . .
        knowingly . . .
            showingly . . .
                goingly . . .
Now he is playing singingly.
    He is playing ringingly, wingingly . . .
        swingingly flingingly tingingly
           faster, faster . . .

He plays busily.
He plays dizzily
He stops.
He mops his brow.
The maestro begins playing again, mildly. . . .
But suddenly he's playing wildly . . .
He bows furiously.
He jabs!
He stabs!
He saws!
He slaps the strings.
He plays trrrr-r-r-i-ppingly.
He plays skippingly . . .
He plays sweepingly . . .
        leapingly . . . cheepingly . . .
            faster . . . faster . . .
He plays nippingly, drippingly . . .
        zippingly . . . clippingly . . . pippingly . . .
            rrrrrriiiiiiiippppppiiinngly . . .
The concert is over.

Here is a book that tells what the Maestro does and how he does it. The sentence pattern that runs throughout the book, noun-verb and noun-verb-adverb, is one that the children will be encountering throughout the course of a lifetime in their speaking and reading and writing. It is a zany story — one that asks to be enjoyed.

1. **Reading joyfully from cover to cover,** p. 78. Invite the children to join in the reading as soon as they have caught on to the story pattern. If you will roll your *r's* and in other ways dramatize your reading, the children will do likewise and you'll all have a lot more fun.

2.
3.
5. **Innovating on literary structure,** p. 79, **Analyzing literary structure,** p. 81 and **Analyzing sentence structure,** p. 87. The children will have no problem borrowing this author's pattern to create their own stories. *The Skater Skates. The Dancer Dances.* You may even end up with *The Teacher Teaches.* As the children discuss the various possibilities for innovations, they will naturally fall into a discussion of the literary structure—the author's way for repeating a basic pattern, his way for using internal rhyme schemes. They will also be discussing the sentence pattern, since the whole story is hung around a sentence pattern.

Won't it be interesting to hear them verbalize their observations about the relationship between the noun and verb in such a sentence as: *The skater skates?* Don't press for exact terminology. The important learning is the children's observation that different kinds of words perform different functions in sentences. This same observation can be made as they look at the adverbs: *He plays skippingly*. They may wish to try their own hands at writing exciting sentences with only three words in each—a naming word, an action word and a describing word. At some point you may get into a discussion of word-order in sentences, observing that when the describing word is used with an action word, it usually follows the word. When a describing word is used with a naming word, it usually comes before the word. For example: *The happy skater skates wildly.*

6.
7. **Analyzing word structure,** p. 90 and **Responding to typographical intrigue,** p. 92. The exaggerated spellings of the adverbs in this story invite much discussion about the fact that words do have shapes. Even mundane considerations such as beginnings and middles and endings of words take on more excitement (and learning!) when they are discussed within the context of typographical intrigue like you find in this book.

8. **Responding to art,** p. 94. The humor and drama and movement in Sal Murdocca's pictures invite long and pleasurable looking and responding on the part of the children. This kind of looking-responding is in itself a mature form of reading.

The Happy Hippopotami

by Bill Martin Jr. with pictures by Bob Velde

The happy hippopotamuses
Climb aboard the picnic buses
For a hippoholiday
In the merry month of May.

    The happy hippopotami
    On the sunny beach do lie
    Like a stretch of granite boulders
    Except, of course, for sunburned shoulders.

        Happy hippopotamamas,
        Wearing pretty beach pajamas,
        Spread tons of cheese on soda crackers
        To feed the hungry crackersnackers.

Happy hippopotapapas
Stroll about the candy shoppas,
Giving children dimes and nickels
To buy their favorite papasickles.

    Happy hippopotadaughters
    Dive into the shallow waters,
    Splashing waves across the ocean,
    Tossing ships in stormy motion.

        Happy hippopotasons
        Fill their trusty "watta" guns
        And gallop out to meet the foe
        That lurks about them row on row.

Happy hippopotapooses,
Toddling boldly on the "looses,"
Stuff the pockets of their britches
With gooey jelly sandywiches.

Happy hippopotamisses
Dance the maypole, throwing kisses
To a crowd of hippymen
Who gaily throw them back again.

Happy hippopotamisters
With hippy hair and hippy whiskers
Gaily strum their steel guitars,
Rock and roll like TV stars.

Happy hippopotapilots
Glide about in eagle "flylets,"
Rising on the sudden breezes
Whenever any hippo sneezes.

Happy hippopotamights
Dressed in polkadotted tights
Compete for hippopotaprizes,
Lifting weights ten times their sizes.

Happy hippopotamezes
Fly about on high trapezes,
Somersaulting through the air,
Acrobatting with a flair.

Happy hippopotapreachers
Call the hippos to the bleachers
To hear a ton of inspiration
And another ton of appreciation.

At last the happy 'potamuses
Climb back aboard the picnic buses
Shouting, "Hip-hippo-ray! Hip-hippo-cheer!
Until we meet again next year!"

If you and the children listen to and take part in the cassette recording of this book done by Bill Martin and Al Caiola in rock rhythm, you will truly have the spirit of the story.

1. **Reading joyfully from cover to cover,** p. 78. If the cassette recording is not available, perhaps you and the children can create your own tune and sing the book from cover to cover. Don't be afraid to try a rock rhythm. The children will help you out.

2. **Innovating on literary structure,** p. 79, **Analyzing literary structure,** p. 81, and **Analyzing rhythmical struc-**

3. **ture,** p. 86. As the children discuss the author's way for putting his story together in preparation for their own innovations,

4. they will notice and verbalize the fact that there is a definite rhyme scheme and rhythmical pattern. They may be able to tell you some of the times when their recognition of where the rhyming words fell helped them decode certain words. This kind of first-hand observing and experimenting with rhyme and rhythm helps the children develop awareness which they will use in their independent reading.

5. **Analyzing sentence structure,** p. 87. Each verse in this zany rhyme can be viewed as a sentence that invites experimentation. Write any one of these sentences across the chalkboard, and invite the children to substitute their own words for each word in the model sentence.

The happy hippopotamuses climb aboard the picnic buses
    wary   children   hid   behind   school fence

for   a   hippoholiday in the merry   month of May.
with   wish   pounding heart   everyone.

As the children substitute nouns for nouns and verbs for verbs, etc., they will be learning much about the function and placement of words in English sentences. Isn't it interesting, for example, that the words *happy* and *merry* come in front of the words they are describing. To place them in another order, would destroy the sound of sense in the sentence.

The children will also learn much about sentences and how they work by rearranging the four segments (chunks of meaning) in each sentence:

In the merry month of May, the happy hippotamuses climb aboard the picnic buses for a hippoholiday.

Recognizing the movable parts and various rearrangements within sentences gives children confidence and versatility for unlocking complex sentences in their independent reading.

ⓒ. **Analyzing word structure,** p. 90. The great play on all of the "hippo" words is a joyous invitation to study the ways words go together.

ⓒ. **Responding to art,** p. 94. The children will enjoy picture-reading this book, responding to Bob Velde's humorous drawings in ways that please them. And don't forget—their chuckles and open merriment are proof of their comprehension of the story.

My Days are Made of Butterflies

by Sano M. Galea'i Fa'apouli adapted by Bill Martin Jr.
with pictures by Vic Herman

My days are made of butterflies
  that gather on the melon vine,

My days are made of oranges
  that ripen in the warm sunshine,

My days are made of sudden rains
  that drench the yard with happiness,

My days are made of hungry hawks
  that stalk the desert wilderness,

My days are made of working
  with my father planting sugar beets,

My days are made of herding lambs
    that wander from our flock of sheep,

My days are made of singing
    in the village at fiesta time,

My days are made of resting
    near the fountain at siesta time,

My days are made of ling'ring
    in the kitchen while my mother cooks,

My days are made of pondering
    the pictures in my storybooks,

My days are made of watching
    for the coming of the school bus,

My days are made of candy
    the piñata showers down on us,

        Then, when the sun
            slips down behind the mountains
            and the silent owl on the nightwind wings,

        I lie looking at the quiet stars
            and wonder what tomorrow brings.

All children, but especially Mexicans and Chicanos, will find themselves personally touched by this gentle account of a child's life in the Southwest.

1. **Reading joyfully from cover to cover,** p. 78. This is not a book that the children will immediately join in on the first reading. It may take two or three readings by you before the children "soak in" the language sufficiently to chime along. Even then it will not be a boisterous reading, as that is not the tone of the book.

2. **Innovating on literary structure,** p. 79. **Analyzing literary structure,** p. 81. **Analyzing rhythmical structure,**

3. p. 86. **Analyzing sentence structure,** p. 87. The children will soon discover that if they are not familiar with the events

4. in this book, the author's pattern for putting the book together will not be especially useful in releasing specific vocabulary.

5. The children who are familiar with these kinds of events will find themselves helped in their reading when they recognize the author's use of rhyme scheme and a simple listing of events. If they clap the rhythm of the sentences, they will see how true it is and can observe how the author could use this underlying rhythmical pattern for selecting certain vocabulary. They can try substituting words with a different number of syllables in various lines to see how important the rhythm is. This kind of insight can be developed into a word-unlocking skill. As the children begin telling and writing their own stories using the "My days are made of ..." pattern, they will come to appreciate how a simple pattern like this can hang a whole story

together and can release vocabulary. They may discuss the fact that in this particular story, it is the basic sentence pattern that gives the story its structure, and they may be intrigued by the fact that transforming the sentence is one way to get a whole new collection of stories going.

My	*days*	*are*	*made*	*of*	*butterflies*
	life	is	colored	with	friends
	soup		flavored		vegetables

that	*gather*	*on*	*the*	*melon*	*vine.*
who	hurry	down		shady	street
which	cook	in		hot	water

6. **Analyzing word structure,** p. 90. Words such as *siesta, fiesta, piñata,* invite a kind of word wonder that may trigger the children into a discussion of what they do and don't notice about the sight and sound of words. Any time children verbalize their first-hand observations about spoken and printed words, they cross-pollinate with one another and sharpen their word-recognition skills.

8. **Responding to art,** p. 94. Vic Herman is recognized by both the Mexican and United States governments as an artist whose paintings have brought feelings of good will to the people of both countries. All of the children and adults who posed for the paintings in this book are Mexican, so the children reading the book can truly have the feeling that they have met some new Mexican friends.

What to Say and When to Say It

captions by Bill Martin Jr. cartoons by Bob Shein

59

Whenever children have fun with the intrigue of language, their love of language and consequently their knowledge about language and how it works improves. This book invites this kind of fun and learning.

1. **Reading joyfully from cover to cover,** p. 78. Invite the children to chime in on the first reading, choosing parts to read or even act out, creating choral reading arrangements, or in any other way enjoying the hilarious situations.

5. **Analyzing sentence structure,** p. 87. The sentences in this book are basic expressions which the children have been hearing all of their lives. It will be interesting for them to discuss how many of the patterns are already stored in their linguistic warehouses from having heard them so often. This can lead to a discussion of how handy it is to have a linguistic warehouse where sentence patterns and story patterns and rhyme schemes can be stored for a lifetime of use. They may wish to make a list of other cultural expressions which seem to belong to all of us ("Happy Birthday!" "I'll be seeing you." Etc.) and create books or comic strips of their own. As they examine the various patterns, you may wish to invite their observations about the punctuation — the use of question mark and period in the question and answer patterns, and especially the use of the comma.

6. **Analyzing word structure,** p. 90. Whenever rhyming words are juxtaposed in intriguing patterns, children are invited to make observations about both the regularities and irregularities of the English language. You may wish to make lists of words which follow a regular pattern and those which don't:

Lou	Marty	Flynn	Fern	peas
you	party	in	turn	Keyes

While they are looking at words and studying their patterns, they might like to think of some of the phonics generalizations they have heard and see how these words do or don't follow the generalization. In a word like *Lou*, for example, or *again* (in the story rhyming with the word *Ben*), is it true that the first vowel does the talking when the two vowels in each of these words "go walking?"

8. **Responding to art,** p. 94. The humor in Bob Shein's drawings is what lifts these cultural expressions out of the mundane. What fun it will be if the children decide to create humorous drawings for otherwise commonplace language. If you are brave, you might invite them to create a book out of certain expressions that are part of your and the children's daily classroom vocabulary. You might be surprised to discover how many classroom expressions are repeated often enough to almost become standardized.

The Turning of the Year

by Bill Martin Jr. with paintings by Samuel Maitin

In January out I go
to welcome winter's icy blow.

In February out I go
to sled on hillsides bound with snow.

In March the warming noontime sun
spells the end of winter's run.

In April springtime calls to me
to splash through puddles recklessly.

In May springtime calls to me
to climb the blossomed apple tree.

In June the warm earth fashions green
while insects sing goodbye to spring.

In July summer calls me come
to taste the ripening wild plum.

In August summer calls me come
to harvest fields that praise the sun.

In September summer calls its ending
with blue haze and chrysanthemums blending.

In October autumn calls me out
to behold the maples' raucous shout.

In November autumn calls me out
to gather pumpkins strewn about.

In December autumn calls its warning,
"Get ready for a winter morning!"

Here is a story that is hung together around familiar cultural sequences (months of the year and seasons) and a rhyme scheme.

1. **Reading joyfully from cover to cover,** p. 78. The children may need to hear several readings of this book before spontaneously chiming in on a cover-to-cover reading. If you invite them to join you whenever they'd like to, they will probably pick up the author's structural clues and read the clusters of words involving the months of the year, the season, and some of the rhyming lines. After a few readings, they will claim this lyrical language as their own and their lives and reading power will be enhanced.

2. **Innovating on literary structure,** p. 79 and **Analyzing literary structure,** p. 81. Since monthly and seasonal pur-
3. suits vary from place to place in our country, the children may wish to borrow the author's monthly and seasonal pattern, filling in their own specifics. There should be no attempt to regiment a child's monthly or seasonal choice. If one child thinks of January as the time for going to basketball games, how nice. Several children may associate the various months with birthday celebrations. Some may even have sad memories that mark some of the months. The important thing for each child to realize is that each of us has a "turning of the year" which gives our lives shape and significance. In creating their own innovations, the children may wish to discuss Bill Martin's

way for using rhyme scheme and the seasonal break in putting his poem together. They may or may not wish to borrow his pattern.

4. **Analyzing rhythmical structure,** p. 86. Most poems that have a dependable rhyme scheme, also have a dependable underlying rhythmical structure. In fact, many poets create the rhythm pattern before selecting the specific vocabulary for their poems. (Interestingly enough, many children go into reading this way. Using hands or feet or head or total body, they respond to the rhythm in a piece of writing long before they latch on to the specific words. Unfortunately, most reading programs do not help teachers recognize and value this important way for going into reading, and the children who skillfully utilize this method are labelled problem readers.) The children may enjoy clapping out the various stanzas to "The Turning of the Year" to see how faithfully the author adheres to a rhythmical pattern. For example, if he had said, "In January, out I travel," his rhyming word at the end of the second line would also need two syllables.

5. **Analyzing sentence structure,** p. 87. The children may be especially interested in the poet's inverted pattern "out I go." In the English language, the subject-verb-adverb order is usually followed, "In January, *I go out.*" For the most part, the poets are the only ones who have enough courage and inventiveness to tamper with the word-order of the English lan-

guage. We ordinary mortals will say, "A pancake is round." The poet will charm us all with, *"Round is a pancake."* The children may touch their own poetic yearnings by transforming a basic inverted sentence:

> *In January, out I go . . .*
> *By evening, home I fly . . .*
> *At four o'clock, out I burst . . .*
> *At mealtime, down I gourge . . .*

8. **Responding to art,** p. 94. You may have children who have never encountered Sam Maitin's kind of art—pictures which evoke feelings and impressions rather than creating an exact picture. Won't it be fun to discuss what ideas come to the children's minds as they study these provocative paintings? And won't it be fun to invite experimentation with this particular use of color and shape? It is important for the children to know that rejecting a particular art form is just as important as selecting it. What really matters is knowing one's choices in art forms and feeling free to experiment.

I Paint the Joy of a Flower

by Bill Martin Jr. with paintings by Carolyn Jablonsky • Helen
Winslow • Hong • C. P. Montague • Stanley Maltzman • R. W.
Davidson • Buffalo Kaplinski • Audrey Menicucci • Ronald
Thomason • Irving Shapiro • Jackson M. Hensley • Howard Bobbs
• Arthur Hall • A. W. Dowl • Frank Riley • Seong Moy

I paint the joy of a flower,
   the flaming of leaves,
   the boldness of mountains,
   the dance of a breeze,
   the aloneness of prairies,
   the break of the sea,
   the silence of summer,
   the age of a tree,
   the circling of seagulls,
   the dusting of snow,
   the lure of the water,
   the blue of shadow,
   the brilliance of aspens,
   the shyness of streams,
   the glory of sunsets,
   the wonder of dreams.

Here is a book that is indeed a miniature art gallery. As you read aloud, allow time from page to page for the children to take in the beauty of the paintings along with the beauty of the lines.

1. **Reading joyfully from cover to cover,** page 78. This is not the kind of book the children will immediately chime in on for a joyous cover-to-cover reading. They may need to hear it several times, taking in the rhyme scheme as well as the rather complex, picturesque language. When they do chime in, it will probably be a reflective reading at first as they experiment with the language.

2. **Innovating on literary structure,** page 79, **Analyzing literary structure,** page 81 and **Analyzing rhythmical**
3. **structure,** page 86. Your reading table can easily come alive with innovations on the basic structure of this story:

4.
> *I sing the joy of a school day ...*
> *I scream the excitement of a ballgame ...*
> *I cherish the happenings at camp ...*

As the children plan their own innovations, they will be deciding whether to stay with a definite rhyme scheme and rhythmical pattern as the author, Bill Martin, did. This may mean figuring out how regularly the second and fourth lines rhyme.

It may also mean clapping out the rhythm of various lines to see how the choice of a two rather than a one syllable word, for example, can change the rhythmical pattern.

> *I paint the joy of a flower . . .*
>
> *I paint the happiness of a flower . . .*
>
> *I discover the beauty of a flower . . .*

Each cluster of words has a definite rhythmical structure, and the children will soon discover their preferences. In matters such as selecting rhyme scheme or rhythmical pattern, luckily there is no right answer. The important consideration is for the children to recognize the differences in the various patterns and to know that these basic structures are just as much a part of the message as the words they choose.

5. **Analyzing sentence structure,** page 87. The children may be intrigued to realize that this entire book is one sentence. This can invite all sorts of experimentation with the basic structure of the sentence. You may wish to write the entire sentence across the chalkboard and then try transforming it (substituting nouns for nouns, verbs for verbs, etc.). What fun for the children to realize that their new sentence is itself a new book. Then you may wish to look at each page of print as a movable part in the sentence and try rearranging them to see what effect this has on the sentence:

I paint the joy of a flower,
the flaming of leaves,
the boldness of mountains,
the dance of a breeze,

I paint the boldness of mountains,
the joy of a flower,
the dance of a breeze,
the flaming of leaves,

All of this kind of experimenting helps children figure out how sentences work in the English language thus helping them gain skill in speaking and reading and writing.

8. **Responding to art,** page 94. You will want to have several sessions with this book where the children respond to the art without thinking about the print. They may be interested to know that all of these paintings are gallery art and they can imagine themselves walking through a famous gallery as they enjoy the paintings and select favorites. They may wish to discuss and experiment with the various styles used by the artists ranging all the way from highly realistic paintings of the natural environment to the highly symbolic sunset which brings the poem to a close. It will be exciting if the children decide to become gallery painters and create a gallery in your classroom or in the corridor. They may even wish to illustrate Bill Martin's poem with their own paintings.

The Eagle Has Landed

by Bill Martin Jr. paintings by Frank Aloise

Ladies and gentlemen,

Here we are at Cape Kennedy. This is the day, July 16, 1969, that man begins his journey to the moon.

10, 9, 8, ignition, 6, 5, 4, 3, 2, 1, 0. All engines running. Lift-off! We have a lift-off!

We are now 2 minutes and 43 seconds into the flight. Apollo 11 has reached an altitude of 217,655 feet, traveling at 6,141 miles per hour. The first stage rocket has done its job! Now it is jettisoned and the second stage rocket takes over.

9 minutes 11 seconds after lift-off! Altitude 609,759 feet, 15,468 miles per hour. The third rocket engine takes over. It's Go! for orbit around the earth!

2 hours, 44 minutes into the flight. Apollo 11 lifts out of earth's orbit at 24,182 miles per hour. Man is on his way to the moon!

3 hours, 15 minutes into the flight. The astronauts release the moon-landing craft from its housing.

They dock the craft at the nose of the command ship and continue the journey to the moon, coasting through space.

July 19   75 hours and 50 minutes after lift-off. A short burn of the rocket engine brakes the speed of Apollo 11 and puts it into orbit around the moon.

July 20   100 hours and 14 minutes after lift-off. The Eagle undocks, carrying two of the three astronauts toward the surface of the moon. The third astronaut pilots the mother ship, the Columbia, in moon orbit.

July 20, 1969   102 hours and 45 minutes into the flight. "The Eagle has landed!"

July 21, 1969   109 hours and 20 minutes into the flight.

Man walks on the moon!

(continued)

(continued)

124 hours and 21 minutes into the flight. **The Eagle rockets off of the moon leaving its landing legs behind.**

127 hours and 55 minutes into the flight. **The Eagle returns to the Columbia for docking.**

The two moon walkers re-enter the mother ship.

July 22

135 hours and 25 minutes into the flight. **Apollo 11 heads earthward, leaving the Eagle in aimless orbit around the moon.**

July 24

Apollo 11 re-enters the earth's atmosphere, falling at 2,950 miles per hour, 4,338 feet per second. Now the astronauts jettison the third stage rocket.

194 hours and 50 minutes after lift-off. **The engineless ship, now a glowing capsule, falls toward the earth at 24,000 miles per hour, and heads for splashdown.**

Splashdown! The capsule is cradled in the Pacific Ocean.

195 hours and 13 minutes after lift-off. **A rescue team reaches the capsule and buoys it up.**

The world's first moon-men are safely home.

The Eagle Has Landed is hung together in a series of time sequences. The astronauts move further and further into the flight until it comes to an end. Your reading aloud of the book may awaken language that has been stored in the children's linguistic storehouses from hearing broadcasts and other discussions of space flights. If so, it will be interesting for the children to read along with you. You may be surprised to discover how much of this technical language the children already own.

2. **Innovating on literary structure,** p. 77 and **Analyzing literary structure,** p. 79.   Once the children have verbalized
3. their understanding of how the author used the passage of time to organize his story, they may be able to think of other stories that have been put together this way. A story doesn't have to have the formal statement about time at the beginning of an episode to move in terms of time sequences. Autobiographies often move this way, for example. So do detective stories and other stories about happenings. Some children may wish to experiment with the formal time statement—varying it to suit the purpose of their stories:

> *We are now one hour into my life. We are now three days into the trip. (The trip being anything from Columbus' voyage to a trip to Oz.)*

5. **Analyzing sentence structure,** p. 87   Sentence patterns in this story range from simple to highly complex. Children will enhance their own collections of sentence patterns as they select favorite sentences to transform.

Man	*walks*	*on*	*the*	*moon.*
Father	*crawls*	*under*		*table.*
Frank	*leaps*	*over*		*fence.*

The engineless ship, now a glowing capsule,
    sightless   child   smiling girl,

falls toward the earth at 24,000 miles per hour,
runs   her friend   2   steps   second,

and   heads   for   splashdown.
                         school.

8. **Responding to art,** p. 95   Help the children verbalize in their own ways, the fact that this is documentary art which was produced from research on the moon trip. They may remember similar paintings depicting the landing of the Pilgrims, the landing of Columbus or other historical events. It may come as something of a relief to your highly visual children to realize that history can be recorded in paintings as well as in words. Invite the children to speculate on which of the paintings in *The Eagle Has Landed* would be likely to be most important 100 years from now.

INSTANT READERS

LEVEL 3 Teacher's Guide

Follow-up activities for Level 3 books

PART 3

1. Reading joyfully from cover to cover

Immediately after reading one of the *Instant Readers* to the children, you will want to invite them to read the book "on their own." This can happen in a variety of ways.

(a) With a dependably structured book like *Ten Little Squirrels*, they will probably chime in long before you come to the last page. As their voices grow louder and louder, they will be proving to themselves and to you that they can read the book. Equally dependably structured but more complex books such as *The Happy Hippopotami* will bring forth this same strong desire to read the book joyfully from cover to cover—a child's sure way for knowing whole-book-success.

(b) You may want to ask, *Children, would any of you like to try reading this book by yourselves?* If you have several copies of the book, so much the better. Give them to the reaching hands, inviting the children to read on their own, read to one another, look over a friend's shoulder to read, and in other spontaneous ways to cement the fact that they can read the book.

(c) Much of the children's read-aloud can turn into choral reading. Invite them to help you decide on various arrangements of chorus and solo parts. Whatever arrangements they decide upon, heart-warming dramatic and esthetic dimensions enter the classroom when choral reading takes the place of the semicircle of children monotonously reading aloud page by page.

(d) Once the children have an *Instant Reader* firmly in their ears, their choral reading can take on the added dimensions of pantomime, dance and other forms of acting out.

(e) It can be useful to have a reading table or reading shelf where sure-fire books for the children's independent reading are kept. Then whenever the children have a free moment, they can select one of these special books to reinforce belief in themselves as readers. These "safe" books gradually become the bridge to the library and the children's wider world of independent reading. They also become the handy resource for ever-maturing language and literary analysis.

2. Innovating on literary structure

When children borrow the underlying structure of a poem or story and hang their own ideas on that structure:

(a) they are having intuitive experiences with the fact that stories and poems do have underlying structures,

(b) they are building a bridge between the linguistic facts of their own worlds and the linguistic facts of the printed page.

The invitation to "write about anything you want to" may fall heavily on the ears of a child who doesn't own the basic language structures to give wings to what he wants to say. On the other hand, a child of seemingly meager vocabulary can latch onto a structure that comes in through his ears and deposits itself indelibly in his mind, and suddenly find his formerly meager vocabulary taking on new dimensions. The *Instant Readers* make it possible for children either of rich or meager vocabulary to find challenge in their new creations which come about as they innovate on the dependable structures found in these books.

Children, supposing you didn't want your days to be made of butterflies? What else might your days be made of?

Children have been known to "tell the stories of their lives" in response to this question, shedding real light on what is and isn't important to them.

And children, supposing you wanted to use the author's idea of having some of the lines rhyme.

It isn't important that the children borrow the author's exact rhyme scheme. Whatever plan for rhyming lines they decide upon, they are recognizing how easily certain words fall into place once a person is aware of the plan for making lines rhyme.

> *My days are made of wishing*
> *that I had a baby brother,*
> *My days are made of keeping*
> *secret secrets from my mother,*

At some point, your room may be filled with reading charts made from innovations worked out by your group. Exploit these charts for all they are worth, inviting children to read them, to analyze how the stories and poems are put together, to identify new words they now recognize, to claim words for their individual wordcard collections.

In addition to new stories and poems worked out by the group, the children will need time and help for creating their own individual innovations. Your reading table may come alive with 15 new books each time you read an *Instant Reader* and invite the children to borrow the structure and to adorn it with their own thoughts and language. What a wonderful source of material for the children's independent reading! When children are on their own reading innovative books that are built on structures which they have already claimed in read-aloud times with the *Instant Readers*, the children will not only be able to read the new books more easily, but they will also be recognizing how useful a person's knowledge about underlying structure can be in helping him read. It is this basic kind of reading know-how that the children carry forward into their library and other independent reading.

$\mathcal{3}$□ Analyzing literary structure

When children realize that a story or poem has a plan back of it and when they recognize the specifics of that plan, they use this knowledge to predict much of the language they encounter in their reading. The *Instant Readers* give children six dependable kinds of literary structure to intake and analyze.

(a) *Repetitive structure.* As children listen to and read books like *Tricks or Treats,*

> *Down to the ninth floor.*
> *Knock on Knicker Knocker's door.*
> *"Tricks or treats?"*
> *"Tricks," says Knicker Knocker.*
> *So I change into a Knocker Knicker.*
>
> *Down to the eighth floor.*
> *Knock on Slipper Slopper's door.*
> *"Tricks or treats?"*
> *"Tricks," says Slipper Slopper.*
> *So I change into a Slopper Slipper.*

they soon catch on to the fact that repetition has a lot to do with the structuring of this story and they find themselves able to read certain phrases and lines because they know from the pattern when the language will repeat.

(b) *Interlocking structure.* In contrast to the structure of *Tricks or Treats?*, those children who have the Level II book, *Old Mother Middle Muddle*, will discover that in this book the episodes do not simply repeat. Rather, they interlock with one another in an intriguing and dependable way:

> *Old Mother Middle Muddle*
> *put down her knitting*
> *and went to the kitchen to brew a cup of tea.*
>
> *"O joy!" said the mouse*
> *"when Old Mother Middle Muddle*
> *makes a cup of tea,*
> *she's sure to have a cookie*
> *and drop some crumbs for me."*

"O joy!" said the cat,
    "when the mouse comes out to eat the crumbs,
        I'll pounce on him!"

"O joy!" said the dog,
    "when the cat comes out to pounce on the mouse,
        I'll bite her."

Once children have caught on to the interlocking nature of the plot structure, they will find themselves able to figure out much of the language in each subsequent episode.

(c) *Familiar cultural sequences.* A book like *Tricks or Treats?* is partly hung together by familiar cultural sequences. The Hallowe'en character begins on the ninth floor and goes down one floor at a time. Simply by living in the culture and intaking ordinal number, the children will read *seventh, sixth,* etc. after hearing the first two episodes. Similarly for *The Turning of the Year.*

In January out I go
    to welcome winter's icy blow.
In February out I go
    to slide on hillsides bound with snow.
In March the warming noontime sun
    spells the end of winter's run.
In April springtime calls to me
    to splash through puddles recklessly.
In May springtime calls to me
    to climb the blossomed apple tree.
In June the warm earth fashions green
    while insects sing goodbye to spring.

81

Once the children have caught on to the fact that this book is partly hung together by the seasons and months, they will be able to place the names of the months and seasons in the appropriate places and read them with ease. This knowledge about the underlying structure of the book will also create a useful readiness for much of the other language in the book, since the children will expect seasonal happenings within each series of seasonal episodes.

(d) *Cumulative structure.* Children who have the Level II book, *Old Devil Wind*, available can deposit another useful literary structure in their linguistic storehouses.

> *One dark and stormy night*
> *Ghost floated out of the wall*
> *And he began to wail.*
>
> *Stool said, "Ghost, Ghost, why do you wail?"*
> *Ghost said, "It is a dark and stormy night*
> *   and so I wail."*
> *And Stool said, "Then I shall thump."*
> *So stool began to thump.*
>
> *Broom said, "Stool, why do you thump?"*
> *Stool said, "It's a dark and stormy night*
> *   and Ghost wails and so I thump."*
> *Broom said, "Then I shall swish."*
> *So Broom began to swish.*
>
> *Candle, said, etc.*

By the time the children have worked their way through the

Broom episode, they are able to predict the pattern of the story. They know that each new episode will carry everything that went in preceding episodes before adding the new happening. Because of this recognition of cumulative literary structure, the children are able to read much of the vocabulary in the book.

(e) *Rhyme scheme.* When children read

> *I paint the joy of a flower,*
> *the flaming of leaves,*
> *the boldness of mountains,*
> *the dance of a breeze,*
> *the aloneness of prairies,*
> *the break of the sea,*
> *the silence of summer,*
> *the age of a tree,*

they sense that the author's way for rhyming the second and fourth of each four lines, will in part help them read the book. In the line *the age of a tree,* for example, they see the picture of a tree and they know that they need a rhyming word with *sea,* and this gives them a reliable clue as to where the word *tree* will fall in the line.

(f) *Time sequences.* Some stories move ahead chronologically. *The Eagle Has Landed* is one of these stories.

> *We are now 2 minutes and 43 seconds*
> *into the flight.*
>
> *. . .*
> *9 minutes 11 seconds after lift-off!*

...
2 hours, 44 minutes into the flight.
...

Once the children discover that each double-page-spread opens with a time statement, and that each time statement carries the reader further into the flight, they will be prepared for much of the language in these opening statements. They will also expect the language in each episode to describe an event that occurred after the event in the previous episode.

After children have had the intuitive experience of reading a book partially because they are able to sense and use the clues given by the underlying structure, it can be useful to help them verbalize their intuitive experience and thus make it available as a decoding skill in future reading. This kind of verbalizing can best be triggered by questions which zero-in on the literary structure rather than the so-called story facts.

> *Children, when did you first hunch that certain lines were going to be repeated again and again in the story?*

> *When did you first hunch that the author was going to use the months and seasons in their regular order?*

> *When did you figure out that there were going to be rhyming words in this book?*

> *When did you figure out in which lines the rhyming words were going to be?*

The children's responses to such questions will not be instantly forthcoming, especially in their early experiences with this kind of analyzing. Neither will they be precisely spoken nor all the same.

> *Well, when the author kept saying, "Down to the ninth floor... Down to the eighth floor..." I knew he was going to keep on saying it that way.*

> *When the second and fourth lines rhymed, I wondered if the poem would keep on rhyming that way and I kept thinking of rhyming words.*

One highly useful way for helping children verbalize their intuitive knowledge is to give them a verbal model for knowing what they know:

> *Isn't this exciting, children? Here you are figuring out the ways authors put their stories and poems together! Have you noticed, children, that the minute you catch on to the author's plan, your reading of a book is easier?*

4. □ Analyzing rhythmical structure

The *Instant Readers* are shot through with rhythm patterns which assist children in recall of sweeps of language and help them decode certain unknown words. By putting them in touch with their own rhythmical impulses, impressionable experiences with these kinds of books help children know that reading involves the entire body, not simply the eyes. For example, once the pattern from the first few pages is in their bloodstream, children will be anticipating the syllabic underpinning of subsequent pages in a story as rhythmically regular as *The Happy Hippopotami*.

The happy hippopotamuses
    Climb aboard the picnic buses
For a hippoholiday
    In the merry month of May.

The happy hippopotami
    On the sunny beach do lie
Like a stretch of granite boulders
    Except, of course, for sunburned shoulders.

The children know that the one-syllable word, *hot,* would not work in the place of the two-syllable word, *sunny.* Nor would the word, *grey,* work instead of *granite.* Just as there are poets who will not write the words of a poem until they have the underlying rhythm, so there are children who keenly respond to the rhythmical pattern of the printed page long before they do to the letter pattern. Unfortunately, many children who do not miss a single beat as they "read with their feet" are not commended for this insightful approach to unravelling print. Instead, they are reprimanded for not sitting still and paying attention to their books. How much better it would be if we recognized this rhythmical response as a significant way for paying attention to one's book and then helped the children add other decoding methods to their growing repertoires.

Many of the *Instant Readers* invite the children to chant and dance and act out as they read. All of these responses help the children add to their knowledge of how language works: it has a rhythm pattern just as surely as it has a spelling pattern. The more familiar children become with the rhythmical underpinnings of language, the more enhanced are their reading and writing skills.

You will notice that after chanting and dancing *The Happy Hippopotami,* children tend not to read the book in word-by-single-word fashion, even when reading alone. The sentences will rise and fall in the natural sweeps of oral language. Morever, you can help the children generalize their first-hand experiences with rhythm into an expectation that rhythm will also be discovered in other stories they read and that the discovery will help them decode print.

5▫ Analyzing sentence structure

Children need to make a go of spoken English sentences if they are to make a go of reading and writing the language. The sentence, not the word, is the basic linguistic unit. The most useful way of figuring out how sentences work is not to fill in countless workbook pages with missing periods and capital letters. Nor is it to memorize rules about how a sentence must have a complete thought. The best way to figure out how sentences work is to have one's head crammed with beautifully constructed sentences that have come in through the ear and are then available for experimentation in figuring out how they were put together.

A basic characteristic of sentences in English is the fact that certain words come in front of certain other words. Young children know this intuitively from learning to talk. At a very early age they may say, "Me hit you," using the incorrect pronoun, but they will not say, "Hit me you," placing the subject pronoun and verb in incorrect order. Simply by living with English speaking people, they have learned the correct word-order for this type of sentence. Similarly, they will say, "pretty girl," rather than, "girl pretty," preferring the sound of the adjective in front of the noun.

The *Instant Readers* offer children a wide-ranging storehouse of sentence patterns. And even with young children, it is productive to engage in a gentle, nondidactic form of sentence analysis. After reading *The Maestro Plays* and after the children have enjoyed reading it on their own several times, you might take a basic sentence pattern:

He plays slowly.

and invite the children to go through the book to see how many other words the author uses to describe the Maestro's playing. This will be one impressionable experience in appreciating the function of adverbs in sentences.

He plays slowly.
        ohly.
        reachingly.
        beseechingly.
        etc.

You may also wish to discuss the position of the adverbs in these sentences.

Isn't it interesting, boys and girls. Whenever Bill Martin uses a word to tell how the Maestro plays, he places that word after the word plays. *How do you think the sentences would sound if he placed the describing words in front of the word* plays?

From here the discussion can go in several directions. The children may wish to try out the various sentences in the book, shifting the position of the adverb. If they conclude that the sentences sound better the way they are written in the book, you may wish to go into an investigation of other sentences containing action words and describing words to determine if the describing words which relate to an action word tend to follow the word. You may also wish to discuss the interesting fact that words which describe naming words tend to precede the word they describe. Keep all such discussions on a discovery level, calling them off if the children seem to lose joy in discovering how printed language works. Gently paced discussions of this sort help children develop decoding skills which stand them in good stead in their independent reading. They develop a feeling for the way words fall into place in English sentences and they use this awareness to help them unlock unknown words.

At some point, the children may wish to transform this basic sentence.

He   *plays*   *slowly.*
       laughs   *loudly.*
       sings   *beautifully.*

Such transforming may lead to discoveries about adverbs that do not end in *ly*.

He plays hard.
He fights well.

If they substitute *We* or *They* for *He*, they may get into an interesting discussion about what happens to the verb when the subject becomes plural. Never promote technical language in these discussions. Let the children find their own ways for describing their language discoveries.

If your children have had a lot of experience with transforming sentences (substituting vocabulary), you may wish to invite them to expand this simple sentence by adding collections of words that belong together (clauses).

He plays slowly while everyone laughs.
when no one is listening.
because people like it that way.

This kind of sentence expanding also helps children appreciate the fact that sentences are not just strings of isolated words, but are related words arranged in various shapes.

The Level III *Instant Readers* offer countless model sentences for transforming and expanding.

Man walks on the moon. (The Eagle Has Landed)

The first one said, "What do I see?"
(Ten Little Squirrels)

My days are made of butterflies
that gather on the melon vine.
(My Days Are Made Of Butterflies)

Gradually the children will be aware of the fact that they own these basic patterns to help them in their independent reading and writing.

6. Analyzing word structure

Children spend much time looking for the exact features of a printed word that teachers guides require them to recognize. When it is time for beginning consonants, for example, a child is out of order if he notices the ending of a word. In contrast to this rigidly organized kind of word analysis, children need some time when they are invited into more spontaneous analyses of the printed page. Regardless of the features of printed words which are being studied at other times during the day and in other reading programs, children need invitations to make far-ranging and highly personal observations about patterns they see in printed words, knowing that all observations will be accepted and respected. Your open-ended questions will trigger such observations.

Children, what do you see interesting about the words on this page? (Accept any observations a child makes. If children identify beginnings and endings and middles of words, fine. If a child tells you, "The word goes like this—duh-duh-duh—," he may be telling you that he is a child who first responds to the underlying rhythm of the language. If a child tells you that the word *worm* is the longest word on the page, he may be telling you that he is a child who sees pictures before he sees letter patterns when examining print. How exciting!)

Let's take a look at all of these words ending in ly (*The Maestro Plays*). *Can anyone remember other words ending in* ly *in our* Instant Readers?

The author of this book really likes to invent words (Tricks Or Treats). *Would you say he has*

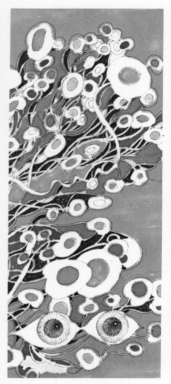

*a plan in mind when he does his inventing or do
you think he just puts down any old letters to
make the new words?* (As the children recognize
the regularity of the plan for changing *Slipper
Slopper* to *Slopper Slipper* and *gum drops* to *dum
grops*, you will have interesting opportunities for
inviting the children into explorations of regularities observed by people who first put the English
language into print. Such a discussion may shed
new light on the children's understandings of
phonic generalizations, inflected endings, etc. It
may also highlight the fact that the English language is not always regular, and this is all to the
good. Recognizing the irregularities of language
is part of appreciating regularities.)

*What do you see interesting about the middles of
some of the words on this page?*

*Who can find the word or words with the most
syllables?* (What a nice time for clapping the underlying rhythm of a page.)

*Let's take a look at our story again and see how
many times the first of two vowels is the one that
is pronounced.*

Hopefully, most of a child's word analysis activities will not be confused with the act of reading. Important though it can be for him to
analyze words that are firmly entrenched in his linguistic storehouse
through hearing and reading stories and poems, *his story books must
not in his eyes symbolize endless drill.* Better to have a time in the

day for word study in its own right. At such a time he can be analyzing word patterns found in his books, but he will not be interrupting the pleasures and linguistic wholeness of his reading. Moreover, if his opportunities for spontaneous word analysis are provided in an atmosphere of enticing discovery rather than rule memorizing, his natural curiosity about printed language will be pleasingly encouraged and this kind of figuring-out-how-printed-language-works will be occurring on an intuitive level all the while he is reading.

From time to time you may wish to offer children word cards, phrase cards, sentence cards and punctuation cards for their personal collections of language reference materials. A shoe box serves handily as a container and what fun the children will have recreating on their own desks, their favorite episodes from *Tricks Or Treats*, adding their own innovations as they go. By the way, when children select especially colorful describing words or action words from their *Instant Readers*, don't be surprised if they follow the typographical invitations in these books and decide on innovative ways for printing the words—including some of the backwards language in *Welcome Home, Henry*. This is one impressive way for confirming their growing knowledge that the visual form of a word is important in reading.

7◻ Responding to typographical intrigue

Somewhere throughout the course of enjoying the *Instant Readers* with the children, you will want to take advantage of the fact that in many of these books the type swells, lurches, screams, whispers, undulates, turns somersaults, and even subsides in pictorial and narrative context. Having type behave in intriguing ways is not foreign to children. We adults have grown accustomed to schoolbooks where the same size and style of type move relentlessly from left to right, page after page, and it is easy to forget that today's children are encountering imaginative and flamboyant uses of type on TV, in magazine advertising and even on their cereal boxes.

Watch the children's faces as they follow the movement of type in *The Maestro Plays.*

He plays trrrrr-r-r-i-ppingly.   He plays skippingly.   He plays sweepingly...

Notice how intently their eyes move with the type. In impressive ways these children are learning the most basic characteristic of type —it moves from one place to another. The sad fact is, most of the early reading programs with their insistence on a rigid left-to-right nonvarying pattern of print, actually cut children off from a fundamental cultural experience which tells children that print is after all a very versatile and exciting invention which to a large degree bends itself to the desires of the user. Rules about beginning on the left and moving to the right are not impressive invitations into the world of print. It is a child's recognition that type moves, a recognition which most easily comes from books where the movement is exaggerated, and his determination to figure out the plan back of the typographical puzzle, that motivate a child to make a go of reading. Once he is caught up in the excitement of following the movement of type as he reads, he will himself come to the generalization that for the most part, type does move from left to right.

You may wish to help children verbalize their adventures with type in the *Instant Readers.* How long was it before they figured out that the word teiuq in *Welcome Home, Henry* is actually the word *quiet* written backwards? Did they have any problems following the dance of the printed words in *Tricks Or Treats?*

> *You children are really getting to be fine detectives when it comes to following type on a page. Perhaps you would like to try writing your own stories with interesting arrangements of words.*

For the psychological advantages as well as for pure enjoyment, from time to time write on the board familiar sentences in reverse directions, in scattered fields of letters, in upright rocketing, in straight downward plunges or in crisscross fashion. Then watch the children delight as they put all of their linguistic skills into the decoding of the language. It is dramatic experiences of these kinds that stand children in good stead as they engage in the less exciting aspects of decoding. Children will work at identifying initial consonants or medial vowels or moving from left to right with more personal determination and pleasure  when they see such activities as part of the larger and more exciting process of figuring out the puzzle of print.

8□ Responding to art

Distinguished art is a hallmark of the Bill Martin books. Each of his series is a wide-ranging art gallery, exposing children to a wide variety of styles, media and design. The *Instant Reader* illustrations include woodcuts, collage, oil, watercolor, poster graphics, crayon, chalk. The range of technique includes cartoon, impressionistic, realistic, abstract, expressionistic. The designs vary from traditional use of type-space-art on a page to flamboyant interrelations that are startling in their unexpectedness. No child will remain passive to the visual aspects of the *Instant Readers*.

You and the children need not worry about the exact terminology as you discuss the art in a book. You can develop the children's awarenesses to styles and techniques in open-ended discussions where you exchange observations and points of view.

Did you ever expect one of your schoolbooks to look like a book of cartoons? (What To Say and When To Say It)

Children, do any of you have any idea about the kinds of feelings you have when you look at Sam Maitin's art? Did you mostly see the snow or did you also feel the wind and the cold? (There are no right answers to such questions. Different children will respond differently. The important thing is opening the children's minds to the notion that lyrical art like that in *The Turning of the Year* can invite various moods by way of feelings.

Children, here is a whole gallery of paintings. Can you choose your three favorites? Knowing what one likes is the beginning of forming taste.